Scotland

Photographs by
Colin Baxter

Text by
Julie Davidson

LOMOND BOOKS
EDINBURGH · SCOTLAND

Scotland

Introduction

From a distance, Scotland is as much a romantic idea as a place on the map. The first 'leisure' travellers who began touring the country in the early nineteenth century (many taking their cue from George IV's extravagant visit to Edinburgh, which turned the traditional dress of the Highlands into a fashion statement) packed their bags with high expectations. Imaginations fired by the historical novels of Sir Walter Scott, souls stirred by the love poems of Robert Burns, these early tourists arrived with the presumption that 'brave Caledonia' would fulfil all their fantasies about 'the land of mountain and the flood'.

Some, inevitably, were disappointed. Any experience of Scotland is bound to be prejudiced by its shifty, sometimes sour weather, and perhaps Sydney Smith saw little but rain and the insides of rank hostelries when he judged it 'the knuckle-end of England – that land of Calvin, oat-cakes and sulphur'. Others, including Charlotte Brontë, praised it, saving their most feverish imagery for Edinburgh. 'Do not think I blaspheme', wrote the novelist to a London correspondent, 'when I tell you that your great London, as compared to Dun-Edin, "mine own romantic town", is as prose compared to

THE CAIRNGORM MOUNTAINS and Loch an Eilein, Rothiemurchus, Strathspey.

EILEAN DONAN CASTLE (opposite) The castle's sentinel site at the confluence of Loch Duich, Loch Alsh and Loch Long has reinforced its reputation as Scotland's most familiar fortress. In fact, the castle's impregnable appearance is deceptive. In the early days of the Jacobite wars Eilean Donan was demolished by the guns of a Hanoverian warship, and was left in ruins until its restoration in the nineteenth century.

LOCH LOMOND
Celebrated in song and literature, studded with islands, Scotland's most famous loch is also the largest body of fresh water in the British Isles. Its east shore is dominated by the shapely mountain of Ben Lomond and spread with the conifers of Queen Elizabeth Forest Park. Despite its proximity to Glasgow, Loch Lomond offers some intimation of Highland wildness.

poetry, or as a great rumbling, rambling heavy epic compared to a lyric, brief, bright, clear and vital as a flash of lightning'.

But the most thoughtful visitors were those whose response was neither depressed nor exalted, but who took the time to appreciate that Scotland can be an acquired taste; tourists like Henry James, for example, whose European travels brought him to Scotland in 1878, when he concluded: 'Once you get the hang of it, and apprehend the type, it is a most beautiful and admirable little country – fit for "distinction" etc., to make up a trio with Italy and Greece'.

'Getting the hang' of Scotland is also the challenge for today's tourists. First-time visitors are likely to arrive with just as many preconceptions and expectations as their nineteenth-century predecessors. They may never have read a Waverley novel or a Burns ballad, but their vision of Scotland will have been shaped by the modern counterparts of Walter Scott and the National Bard: Hollywood film producers, tourist board copywriters, the marketing directors of whisky distilleries, and other agents of popular culture, consumerism and the leisure industry.

Their superlatives may be less creative and more commercial, but their Scotland is also 'brave Caledonia!' and 'the land of mountain and the flood'. Theirs is also a Scotland of cherished traditions and romantic icons: clan gatherings and cottage industries, warrior heroes and tragic queens, Highland games and kilted pipers, heather and hills, lochs and glens – all the elements which down the centuries have given Scotland the robust identity that sets it apart from England.

True, many of the symbols of that identity may be a peculiar mix of marketing emblems, sentimental stereotypes and historical distortions – and some Scots dislike their stranglehold on the tourist industry. But, love it or loathe it, the kilt wrapped around the Scottish identity has become a kind of corporate logo, representing not only the people of the Highlands and Islands but their Lowland kin; and it is possible to argue that tartan has played its part in reinforcing that idea of nationhood which led in 1999 to the recovery of the Scottish Parliament, nearly 300 years after it was lost to the Act of Union with England.

THE RED CUILLIN, ISLE OF SKYE
These are smaller siblings of the island's fearsome Black Cuillin, and their dramatic leap from the shores of Skye's eastern seaboard provides hearty exercise for hillwalkers.

BRAEMAR HIGHLAND GATHERING
Masssed pipe bands feature at this annual Deeside event.

Most first-time visitors, however, will be less interested in collecting evidence of Scotland's dynamic present than exploring its dramatic past. Does the Scotland of their expectations still exist? Will they find the crumbling castles, shining islands and beguiling wilderness of their imaginations? In abundance, and with some ease.

Most of Scotland's five-and-a-half million people live in the central belt, or Central Lowlands, between and around Glasgow and Edinburgh; the infrastructure of its modern economy is concentrated there, or dispersed to the east-coast cities of Dundee and Aberdeen, which means that change lies lightly on the rest of the country. Two or three hours' drive from the central belt brings you under the thrall of the West Highland seaboard and the timeless spell of the Hebrides. The Border hills, with their quiet corners, secretive waters and medieval strongholds are even closer, while each of Scotland's great estuaries – Clyde, Forth and Tay – are gateways from their port cities to an alluring rural hinterland.

HIGHLAND COW
The hardy Highland cow is now more decorative than productive, and is a familiar feature of many farms and estates.

LOCH NEVIS,
WEST HIGHLANDS
(opposite)
The seawaters of the 'loch of heaven', as its name means, form the southern boundary of Knoydart – the most isolated peninsula in the West Highlands.

Scotland is a visual feast, which is why photographs serve its landscape more effectively than words. This book has been organised to help you find your way to its most rewarding features. You will not necessarily follow all or even most of its signposts, but the themes of each chapter – cities, rivers and their hinterland, seaboard, islands and Highland highlights – will give some idea of the character and diversity of this 'beautiful and admirable little country'.

Scotland may not have the climate of Italy or Greece, but its volatile weather is as much a theatrical part of its landscape as sunshine is to the Mediterranean basin. And 'getting the hang' of Scotland, come rain or shine, is a rich adventure.

On the Waterfront

EDINBURGH

Robert Louis Stevenson, who was born here, called the capital 'my precipitous city.' Like Rome, it is built on seven hills – none more precipitous than the centrepiece of Edinburgh Castle. This magnificent view is from Salisbury Crags, looking to the west and Corstorphine Hill. The highest of the seven is Arthur's Seat, a steep but easy climb which opens up vistas around the Edinburgh compass.

The Four Cities

If you ask the citizens of Edinburgh and Glasgow, Dundee and Aberdeen what they have in common their immediate reflex is to say 'Nothing.' Intercity rivalry exists in other countries, but in Scotland – where there are only four cities with populations over 150,000 – the rivalry is as much a gut reaction as a civic pastime.

There is a long history of tension between the largest city, Glasgow (population 625,000) and the capital, Edinburgh (500,000), while the two east coast ports of Aberdeen (200,000) and Dundee (190,000) are locked in economic competition to service the North Sea oil industry. Each is also a regional capital, and their separate characters reflect Scotland's rich mix of dialects and idioms. Aberdeen and Dundee are only 70 miles (110 km) apart, but their citizens speak a different kind of English. Glasgow and Edinburgh are even closer, but the short vowels of Edinburgh's accent become the trailing cadences of Glaswegian speech in the space of 40 miles (65 km).

The proximity of all four makes for intense relationships, and despite the rivalries they have shared much down the centuries – not least a maritime history. Each has evolved around rivers, and two sit on the littorals of mighty estuaries. Glasgow's River Clyde was the gateway to trade with the West Indies and the Americas in the eighteenth century and the powerhouse of Scotland's industrial revolution in the nineteenth century, when the city earned the title of 'Second city of the Empire'. Even into the mid twentieth century the description 'Clyde-built' was synonymous with great feats of engineering and shipbuilding.

After these heavy industries went into decline Glasgow was left with a treasurehouse of glorious Victorian architecture and some of the worst post-industrial slums in Europe. In the 1960s, however, the city embarked on a radical programme of redevelopment and has re-invented itself. Today, it is the style capital of Scotland. In 1990, it became European City of Culture and in 1999 it was UK City of Architecture. Tourists, who once ignored it, now have it firmly in their sights.

GLASGOW FROM THE AIR
The River Clyde was first the commercial and then the industrial powerhouse of the city whose name is said to mean 'dear green place'. When trade opened up with the Americas and the West Indies the Clyde dispatched its merchant ships to bring home fortunes in tobacco, sugar and rum. When the nineteenth century brought industry to Glasgow, Clyde-built steam ships and locomotives were exported all over the world.

EDINBURGH OLD TOWN ROOFTOPS
Looking east towards the Balmoral Hotel and Calton Hill.

WATER OF LEITH, EDINBURGH
The narrow river debouches into the Firth of Forth at the port of Leith. Its redeveloped waterfront has become a fashionable place for restaurants, pubs and housing.

Edinburgh, in the east, looked to Europe rather than the New World for trade. The city by the Firth of Forth has its own port, although the people of Leith, which was an autonomous burgh until the 1920s, still consider themselves 'Leithers'. Leith also had a fleet of deepsea trawlers, and at the end of the nineteenth century began large-scale whaling in the waters of the Antarctic. (This is one of the reasons why Edinburgh Zoo has a world-class collection of penguins.)

Today the vitality of the port is a ghost of its past, but it has had a boost from the North Sea oil industry and, more recently, the regular arrival of cruise ships. The waterfront, once bustling and brawling, has been transformed, not least by the new offices of the Scottish Executive, headquarters of Scotland's administration, and the development of an 'ocean terminal' for the cruise industry.

Some of Edinburgh's best restaurants, liveliest wine bars and most desirable housing have taken over prime sites beside the miniature estuary of Edinburgh's other river, the Water of Leith. This narrow waterway finds such a secretive channel from its source in the Pentland Hills through the city that at times it seems to disappear altogether. But in the eighteenth century it was critical to Edinburgh's

economy, supplying power and water to bleach and dye works, tanneries, and paper, flour and timber mills. Today its banks have been turned into pleasant walkways and cycle tracks, and its passage through the Dean Village, near the west end of Princes Street, is a spectacular gorge spanned by the elegant bridge of Thomas Telford.

Aberdeen, on the exposed coast of the North Sea, has not one river but two running through it. The earliest part of the city, with its ancient cathedral and university, lies on the banks of the less distinguished. While the River Don has been celebrated by its more perceptive enthusiasts and valued by 'a people conditioned to counting wealth in good farming land', as the north-east writer Cuthbert Graham maintained, its reputation has suffered from the greater celebrity of the River Dee. When Queen Victoria bought the Balmoral estate and re-built Balmoral Castle, the river valley acquired the title of 'Royal Deeside'. It has been annually visited by the British royal family ever since.

The Dee estuary also provided the city with its harbour. In the early 1970s the exploitation of oil fields under the North Sea by multinational companies turned that harbour from trading and

ABERDEEN FROM THE AIR
The 'granite city' was built from the stone of one massive quarry, and evolved around the estuaries of two rivers. The oldest part of the city stands on the banks of the River Don, while the River Dee gave Aberdeen its substantial fishing harbour – now shared with vessels of the North Sea oil industry.

RRS DISCOVERY,
DUNDEE
The return of the Antarctic research ship to its home port gave a boost to the economy of the east-coast port, and marked the beginning of a local tourist industry. The 'Discovery Experience' at the Victoria Docks describes many of the Discovery's historic voyages, including Captain Scott's journeys to the polar regions of the southern hemisphere.

fishing port into dynamic docklands; and the austere but self-confident 'granite city', with its industrious, pragmatic people, has been reaping the rewards ever since. Fortunately this economic boom has had little impact on the durable character of the city centre, which dates from the early nineteenth century.

Arguably Dundee has the most splendid site of any of these port cities, and its position on the comely Tay estuary, with the backdrop of an extinct volcano, has given it the sobriquet of 'Naples of the North.' Unlike Naples, however, Dundee destroyed much of its historic legacy in the 1960s and 1970s with a series of developments.

Yet its past was vigorous; before the industrial revolution it was the centre of the Scottish wine trade and a leading importer of French claret, and when the age of steam arrived it was quick to seize initiatives in shipbuilding, textiles and, most famously, the processing of jute from the plantations of the Empire. Marketed as 'the City of Discovery', Dundee is now making the most of its maritime past with a series of tourism initiatives at the Victoria Docks.

The royal research ship *Discovery* was built in Dundee in 1901,

and the imaginative 'Discovery Experience' explains how she took the explorer Captain Scott on his first voyage to the Antarctic. Returned to her home port, she shares the waterfront with HMS *Unicorn* which, built in 1824, is the oldest British-built warship still afloat and one of only four frigates left in the world.

For all their individual merits, it's impossible not to prioritize when directing the visitor towards urban Scotland. Edinburgh is self-selecting; its incomparable city centre, where the medieval Old Town looks across the green valley of Princes Street Gardens to the Georgian New Town, its feast of history, its status as capital and its international arts festival make it the most visited city in the United Kingdom outside London.

EDINBURGH SKYLINE
Across Princes Street Gardens, the tenements of Edinburgh's Royal Mile share their profile with the Assembly Hall and the Bank of Scotland.

CHARLOTTE SQUARE, EDINBURGH
The jewel in the crown of Edinburgh's Georgian New Town.

The mere act of walking around Edinburgh's compact centre opens up one of the most visually dramatic cityscapes in the world, a place of crags and chasms, dark alleys and elegant squares, towering pinnacles and noble domes, sudden glimpses of hill and sea. 'It is totally unlike anything else I have seen,' opined Queen Victoria, after her first visit in 1840.

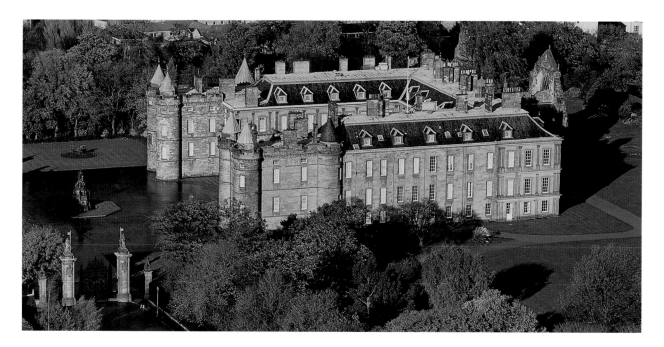

The Old Town on its spiky ridge beneath Edinburgh Castle is the face of Scotland's brutal Middle Ages. Here, the Royal Mile, which links the castle to the Palace of Holyroodhouse, holds the memory of a violent past – easily imagined in the shadowy passageways of its labyrinthine 'closes'. The eighteenth-century New Town, designed by James Craig and embellished by Robert Adam, is the face of the Enlightenment, of the philosopher David Hume, the economist Adam Smith and the writer Walter Scott – the city which became known as 'the Athens of the North.'

The visitor will want to march down the centuries with Edinburgh's past: explore the great castle, parts of which have stood on its volcanic rock since the twelfth century; tour the fifteenth-century Holyrood Palace, with its poignant relics of Mary Queen of Scots and its official status as the present Queen's Scottish residence; climb the Scott Monument, the curious Gothic monolith on Princes Street which was raised as a memorial to the novelist; wander through Holyrood Park and up Arthur's Seat, the miniature mountain which supremely dominates this city of hills, steps and precipitous streets.

But neither should the visitor ignore Edinburgh's present, which has been given a shot in the arm by the opening of the Scottish Parliament, its powers devolved from the UK parliament in London after years of campaigning. (It meets, at the moment, in the Church of Scotland's Assembly Rooms on the Mound, but an innovative, purpose-built chamber is under construction on the edge of Holyrood

THE PALACE OF HOLYROODHOUSE, EDINBURGH
The official Scottish residence of the Queen, the palace has its origins in a twelfth-century abbey. It became a royal palace in the sixteenth century.

EDINBURGH CASTLE
(opposite)
The city's most famous landmark is a multi-purpose complex dating from the twelfth to twentieth centuries. It combines the function of a major tourist attraction with those of British Army barracks and stage for the annual military tattoo. It is also the repository of the Scottish crown jewels and the Stone of Destiny, on which Scottish monarchs were crowned.

WEST END, GLASGOW
As the city expanded west in the nineteenth century, its architects produced some of the finest Victorian buildings in Britain.

THE 'ARMADILLO', GLASGOW
A striking extension to the Scottish Exhibition and Conference Centre.

Park.) Edinburgh's impressive range of national art galleries and museums was supplemented in 1998 by the opening of the striking Museum of Scotland. Built beside the Victorian Royal Museum in Chambers Street, it is a stunning showcase for Scotland's antiquities and historical treasures, which have been liberated from storage.

Glasgow, meantime, continues to polish up its own distinguished architectural heritage. Although the city's origins are ancient – there was a religious community on the north bank of the Clyde in the sixth century – it has few remnants of its medieval history. The oldest surviving house is the fifteenth-century Provand's Lordship, now a museum, and its fine thirteenth-century cathedral managed to escape destruction during the Scottish Reformation. Its eighteenth-century buildings, however, reflect the wealth of an adventurous merchant class who made fortunes through importing tobacco, rum and sugar from the British colonies; while its triumphant nineteenth-century buildings – notably the City Chambers in George Square and the dense grid of streets to its west – show the city at the apotheosis of its Victorian achievements.

Glasgow's instinct and appetite for aspirational architecture continue to this day. Its most celebrated designer at the turn of the twentieth century was Charles Rennie Mackintosh, whose significance to the Art Nouveau movement can be traced throughout the city: Glasgow School of Art, the Willow Tea Rooms, the House for an Art Lover, Scotland Street School, The Lighthouse and the complete reconstruction of Mackintosh's house in the Hunterian Art Gallery. The city's modern architecture is equally audacious – from the purpose-built Burrell Museum, which houses one of Scotland's most visited art collections, to the riverside 'Armadillo', the extension to the Scottish Exhibition and Conference Centre designed by Sir Norman Foster.

Even the culturally indifferent, however, must sense in Glasgow the renaissance of a great city; if only through the style of its designer boutiques and innovative shopping

GLASGOW CITY CHAMBERS AND GEORGE SQUARE

WALL DETAIL, ROOM DELUXE, WILLOW TEA ROOMS, GLASGOW
A unique Charles Rennie Mackintosh interior.

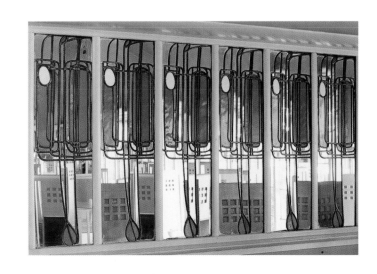

malls and the vitality of its pubs, clubs and restaurants. While Glasgow continues to envy Edinburgh's monopoly of Scotland's institutions, including the devolved parliament, it still has the capacity to make the capital look small-town.

Aberdeen may lack the scale and excitement of Glasgow and the pageantry of Edinburgh, but it refuses to be ignored. Built from the rock of one massive granite quarry (Rubislaw Quarry was once the largest man-made hole in Europe) the city is uncompromising in its own stout view of itself. 'Aberdeen to Heaven, nae a great step' is a local sentiment. Aberdonians don't much care if visitors like their city or not; it's enough that they themselves find much to admire in its cold, clean stone and civic accomplishments.

The city certainly deserves

TOWN HOUSE CLOCK TOWER, ABERDEEN
This mock-baronial timepiece is a familiar landmark on Union Street, the main thoroughfare of a city centre which was designed in the early 1800s and offers easy access to the busy harbour and aromatic fish market.

more than an overnight stop *en route* to Deeside. Aberdeen was already a busy port when it was granted a royal charter in the twelfth century by King William the Lion, but its earliest settlement was clustered around St Machar's Cathedral in Old Aberdeen, once an independent burgh. The cobbled streets, narrow lanes, and medieval buildings beside the River Don remain a peaceful enclave within the modern city and although Marischal College, in the city centre, is the largest granite building in the world after Spain's Escorial Palace, it lacks the weathered dignity and leafy setting of King's College, founded in Old Aberdeen in 1495.

Many of Aberdeen's attractions are within walking distance of Union Street, the imposing, mile-long thoroughfare which the city

fathers commissioned in the early 1800s: Provost Skene's House, whose period rooms span 200 years of design, the busy harbour and the fish market (Scotland's largest) and the exposed beach, whose fine sands are better suited to dog-walking than sunbathing. The city's bracing character and chilly granite are relieved, however, by its sumptuous gardens and parks – not to mention the year-round floral displays that have repeatedly swept the board in national competitions.

The memorabilia of Dundee's maritime history include a whaling exhibition at the Broughty Ferry Museum, in the attractive waterfront suburb of Broughty Ferry. The city had a high reputation for the building of clippers and whalers which, around the turn of the century, were sent north to fish the waters of the Arctic. And although, otherwise, Dundee has little to offer history-conscious tourists, it does have some fascination for students of railway history. The Tay Bridge Disaster is visibly recalled in the forlorn piers of the Victorian railway bridge, which collapsed beneath a night train at the height of a tempest in 1879. All the passengers and crew died in the dark waters of the estuary.

The replacement railway bridge, now supplemented by a road bridge, strides spectacularly across the Firth of Tay, and in the view from the estuary's southern bank Dundee redeems itself.

DUNDEE AND THE TAY BRIDGES
Dundee's site is on the Firth of Tay, where the city climbs the slopes of an extinct volcano. The modern town has a long maritime history as a thriving port, and is also known for its rail and road bridges. The present rail bridge replaces the Victorian structure whose flaws caused a notorious rail disaster in 1879.

Sources of Splendour

Rivers, Estuaries and their Hinterland

The Scottish word for estuary is 'firth' and the geological forces that shaped Scotland's coastline have endowed it with five great estuarial bites and several smaller ones. Three of the main firths are also the mouths of three famous rivers: the Clyde, the Forth and the Tay. Four lesser rivers, the Esk, the Annan, the Nith and England's River Eden, debouch into the Solway Firth, while the Moray Firth is the final outcome of two smaller estuaries fed by the rivers Ness and Beauly.

WHITEADDER WATER, BORDERS
A tributary of the Tweed, this charming little river is one of the region's more secretive waterways.

Each of these firths, and their rivers, are natural conduits to very different hinterlands. The east-coast firths, like the coast itself, are less indented than the complex west-coast estuaries; the Solway and Moray firths are the most rural, with the sandiest littorals; the Clyde and Forth, nipping the waist of the central belt, are the most industrial; and the River Tay, Scotland's longest and, arguably, loveliest river, has a varied career as a sporting and working river between its Perthshire source and its North Sea mouth, as do the celebrated rivers of Tweed and Spey, which flow through splendid Border and Highland scenery respectively. Their estuaries may be unimpressive but their waters provide some of the best fishing in Scotland as well as important employment: textile and woollen mills in the Tweed valley, malt whisky distilleries in Strathspey. The upper valley of the River Dee, in Aberdeenshire, is best known for its royal connections, although the development of the rivermouth at Aberdeen gave that city its harbour.

But the mightiest river of all, in terms of reputation and impact, is the Clyde. It is also the most surprising. The waters which powered Scotland's heavy industry and sent ships and steel throughout the world also water the pastures, orchards and nurseries of South Lanarkshire, and have their springs in the lonely Lowther Hills. If you follow the Clyde from its source to its massive estuary you see Scotland in miniature: from the shapely hills of the Borders through

RIVER AVON & GLEN AVON, MORAY (opposite)
Scotland's rivers flow with some of the purest waters in Europe. They are not only beautiful but productive, challenging anglers with their populations of trout and salmon and supplying one of the ingredients of fine malt whiskies.

the leafy valleys and the towns of the central belt to the Highland landscape of the Firth of Clyde, with its islands, peaks and long sea-lochs.

You also follow the course of much of Scotland's social history, as well as some key landmarks in its centuries of political turmoil. The Clyde is little more than a shallow stream until it nears the ancient Royal Burgh of Lanark, where it grows in volume before plunging over the Falls of Clyde. Lanark remains a town of character, with strong associations with the freedom fighter William Wallace. He is said to have lived in the Castlegate and hidden in a cave in the Cartland Crags, just outside the town, after killing an English soldier in a brawl. But these days it is the former cotton-spinning village of New Lanark that attracts visitors. This little community in a steep glen beneath the Falls of Clyde was the

UPPER CLYDE VALLEY, LANARKSHIRE
The countryside of the Upper Clyde Valley is characteristically open and populated with small communities. With its rolling moorlands and fertile valleys, agriculture plays an important part of the rural scene.

scene of one of the most visionary social experiments of the age of industry. In the early eighteenth century a cotton manufacturer called Robert Owen built houses for his mill workers, opened a free school and operated a co-operative store to clothe and provision them. All the old buildings have been restored as housing, shops, craft workshops and visitor centre, and New Lanark has become one of the most successful tourism initiatives in central Scotland.

From there the river advances prettily between high wooded banks, through orchards and market gardens. Near the village of Crossford it passes close to one of Scotland's best-preserved medieval castles. Craignethan Castle, a stronghold of the Hamiltons (fierce friends of Mary Queen of Scots) was built between the fifteenth and sixteenth centuries and claims to be the original Tillietudlem, which features in Sir Walter Scott's *Old Mortality*.

The Clyde swells with purpose as it passes through the industrial heartland of North Lanarkshire, where the coalmines, steel mills and manufacturing workshops have been largely replaced by light industry and advanced technology plants. Its pulse beats in the centre of Glasgow, where its waterfront is slowly acquiring the apparatus of commerce, housing and leisure.

Clyde ships are still being built in the few remaining yards but the launch of a ship, once commonplace, is now rare. The most regular traffic in the firth is provided by the ferries, which ply from coast to coast and serve the islands of Arran, Bute and Great Cumbrae. Arran is the largest and most spectacular, and its mountains, villages and fourteenth-century Brodick Castle deserve more than a day trip; although it can be visited in a day from the ferry point at Ardrossan.

The north coast of the Clyde estuary is fissured with a bewildering series of narrow sea-lochs, each banked with hills and forests: an adventure playground for walkers, climbers and sailors on the doorstep of Glasgow. By contrast, the Firth of Forth is a simple affair and the River Forth a modest stream, which begins its journey to the North Sea at Aberfoyle, in Stirlingshire. Its most striking feature is the length of its estuary – 51 miles (82 km) – which begins to widen a few miles east of Stirling.

Stirling's position at the highest navigable point of the Forth, together with its massive defensive rock, gave it huge importance in Scotland's wars of independence. Stirling held the pass to the

ISLE OF ARRAN FROM BUTE
The two main islands of the Firth of Clyde supplement their local economies, mainly farming, forestry and fishing, with incomes from tourism. Arran, the largest island in the estuary, is sometimes called 'Scotland in miniature', as its glens, woodland, coast and striking mountain ridges represent all the principal features of Scotland's geography. Low-lying Bute has gentler scenery, fine beaches, and its pleasant capital Rothesay was once a popular destination for urban Scots, who found going 'doon the water' on Clyde steamers breezy relief from their industrial environment.

SCOTTISH PATRIOTS
William Wallace and Robert
the Bruce are remembered in
the Wallace Monument
(above) and 'The Bruce' statue
at Bannockburn (below).

Highlands, and from the battlements of Stirling Castle – arguably the most magnificent fortress in Scotland – you can see seven battlefields; among them, the site of the Battle of Stirling Bridge, when William Wallace's defeat of the English army in 1297 paved the way for the decisive victory at nearby Bannockburn in 1314. This strategic triumph for Robert the Bruce guaranteed Scottish independence for the next 400 years.

With its sixteenth-century walls, built to protect Mary Queen of Scots from the English Henry VIII, Stirling's Old Town is not to be missed. From its high, cobbled viewpoints on the rock you can look across central Scotland, with the Gothic landmark of the Wallace Monument on its site below the Ochil Hills and, to the north and west, the mountains of the Trossachs leaping up from the lowland plain. There is no more graphic demonstration of Stirling's claim to the title 'Gateway to the Highlands'.

You can also trace the coils of the Forth which loop through an industrial-rural spectacle as the river journeys to the sea: the blazing forest of flare-stacks at the port of Grangemouth, centre of a vast petrochemical plant, the well-preserved ruins of the Palace of Linlithgow, birthplace of Mary Queen of Scots, the ancient villages of South Queensferry and Cramond, and the two great bridges that

link the Lowlands to the Kingdom of Fife, each a splendid symbol of the technological achievements of its age.

Beyond Edinburgh and its eastern suburbs of Musselburgh and Portobello (once independent burghs) the firth's littoral takes on the aspect of the seaside. The coast of Fife, to the north, becomes more and more distant and the south coast is fringed with sandy beaches and breezy golf links. The county of East Lothian is famous for golf, pretty villages, rich farmland, small, unspoiled resorts with long histories (Gullane, North Berwick, Dunbar) and handsome ruins (the castles of Dirleton and Tantallon). As the estuary becomes the sea the deserted islands of the Forth reach their apotheosis in the Bass Rock, a monolith of volcanic rock which boasts one of the world's largest gannetries.

The Solway Firth attracts more birdlife than most. South-west Scotland's deep coastal indent and western border with England is a

THE BASS ROCK,
EAST LOTHIAN
Whitewashed with its famous colony of gannets, this uninhabited island is an outstanding landmark in the Firth of Forth.

GANNET

SWEETHEART ABBEY,
DUMFRIESSHIRE
The graceful sandstone ruins
of this thirteenth-century
abbey near Dumfries are
a testament to marital
devotion. It was founded
by the noble Devorguilla
Balliol, who also founded
Balliol College, Oxford,
in memory of her husband,
John. After his death she
carried his heart with her
everywhere, and had it
buried with her own body
under the high altar.

series of shallow bays and tidal sands. The marshlands, mudflats and sandbanks created by its four rivermouths are feeding grounds for wildfowl, and the entire Spitsbergen population of barnacle geese winters on the Solway – notably at Caerlaverock Castle and National Nature Reserve on the Nith estuary.

The Solway's Scottish heartland is the fertile pastures, lonely hills and handsome, black-and-white villages of Dumfries and Galloway. (Its south coast belongs to Cumbria, in England.) This is one of the most rewarding regions in Scotland, but it is often bypassed by visitors hurtling north on the M74, where the main attraction is Gretna Green. This village was once the first available community where couples eloping from England could take advantage of Scotland's different marriage laws. The ceremonies were performed in an old smithy which, sitting among coach parks and souvenir shops, is now a major tourist draw.

Dumfries and Galloway is not only well endowed with beauty and tranquillity, but rich in history. At Whithorn, near Wigtown Bay, Christianity came to Scotland when St Ninian, a local man, built the first Christian church in 397, after a pilgrimage to Rome. At Dundrennan Abbey, near Kirkcudbright, Mary Queen of Scots is believed to have spent her last night in Scotland before her fatal flight to imprisonment in England. And throughout the region there are sombre monuments to the Covenanters, victims of Scotland's religious struggles in the seventeenth century.

Capital of the region is Dumfries, an ancient Border town with a waterfront on the River Nith and the dignified sobriquet of 'Queen of the South.' It has strong associations with Robert Burns. Although the farmer-poet was born in Ayrshire, he took over Ellisland Farm

some 6 miles (10 km) from Dumfries and, when it failed, moved into town to become an exciseman. Ellisland, where he wrote 'Tam O' Shanter' and 'Auld Lang Syne', is now a museum, as is the house in Dumfries where he died in 1796.

Dumfries has a fine town centre, and its position 20 miles (32 km) west of the M74 makes it a natural gateway to the more remote west of the region, with its wild Galloway hills and great bays. East of the M74 another river takes up the turbulent Borders story, which is inseparable from Scotland's centuries of conflict with England. On its comely progress from Tweeddale to the North Sea, the River Tweed passes through or near every important Borders town before turning into the Scottish Border itself near the English town of Berwick-upon-Tweed.

The dales and waters of that other Border barricade, the Cheviot Hills, may be less spectacular than the glens and lochs of the Highlands, but they are often emptier; and the whole region is crowded with evidence of the mixed fortunes of the great Border families —sturdy castles, magnificent stately homes and eloquently ruined abbeys. In the ancient towns of Jedburgh, Melrose,

ETTRICK, BORDERS
The poet and novelist James Hogg (1770-1835), 'The Ettrick Shepherd', was born in the village near here.

SMAILHOLM TOWER, NEAR KELSO, (below)
is the pre-eminent Borders tower. This sixteenth-century defensive construction has many associations with Sir Walter Scott.

*THE RIVER TWEED
AT ABBOTSFORD
The former home of Sir
Walter Scott is now a
literary shrine. Here
the prolific 'Wizard of the
North' wrote* Ivanhoe,
The Heart of Midlothian,
The Bride of Lammermuir
*and all the other historical
novels in the Waverley
canon – not so much under
pressure from deadlines as
pressure from creditors.
Although he tried hard to
turn himself into the Laird
of Abbotsford, Scott couldn't
make his Borders estate pay.*

and Kelso you can trace their histories; and in the equally old but
more industrialised towns of Galashiels, Selkirk and Hawick you find
the residue of the Tweed valley's economy – wool and textile mills.

In the Tweed valley there are also legacies of two of Scotland's
most famous writers. John Buchan, author of *The Thirty-Nine Steps*,
spent childhood summers in Tweeddale, and in the village of
Broughton, near the pleasant town of Peebles, there is a small
museum dedicated to his life and work; and on a grander scale
Abbotsford House, between Selkirk and Galashiels, is a shrine to Sir
Walter Scott, who wrote all the Waverley novels in his Borders home
while trying to turn himself into the Laird of Abbotsford.

Anglers will have their preferences, but it's fair to say that the
Tweed, the Spey and the Tay all have claims to the title of Scotland's
finest salmon-fishing river. The Tay begins life in the heart of
Perthshire, debouching from Loch Tay and finding a route through
glens and gorges to the little towns of Aberfeldy and Dunkeld.
Whether watering broad meadows or reflecting the colours of
Perthshire's glorious broadleaf woods it is always a handsome river,

and by the time it reaches Perth it is
a substantial one. East of the town,
at its confluence with the River
Earn, it begins to swell into the firth,
and passes under its two longest
bridges at the city of Dundee.

The Tay's hinterland is always
interesting, sometimes spectacular.
In Perthshire it keeps company with
some shapely mountains, and
provides the centrepiece of one of
Scotland's most attractive and
important towns. Perth, which lies
in a bowl of wooded hills, was once
the capital of medieval Scotland, and
its ancient status is reflected in the
dignity of its oldest buildings.

North of the river, in what is
virtually a suburb of Perth, is Scone
Palace, which stands on the site of an
abbey destroyed by militant
Protestants in 1559. Between the
ninth and thirteenth centuries Scone
was the custodian of the Stone of
Destiny, on which Scottish kings and
queens were crowned. After a chequered history this sacred stone,
which spent centuries in London's Westminster Abbey, was returned to
Scotland in 1996 and is now in the safekeeping of Edinburgh Castle.

The Fife coast of the Tay's estuary is pleasantly rural, with low,
billowy hills and waterfront villages which have become commuter
satellites of Dundee. To the north, the city of 'jute, jam and
journalism' rises up the conical Law, saving its best-kept secrets for
those who take the time to explore the county of Angus.

The Angus farms lie in the shelter of the southern wall of the
Grampian massif, which is breached by three long, secluded glens.
The single-track roads of Glen Isla, Glen Prosen and Glen Clova lead
to prime hill-walking country, with clusters of Munros – mountains
over 3000 ft (914 m) – and old drove roads which once linked the
markets of Angus with the cattle farms of Aberdeenshire. The little

*THE RIVER TAY
AT PERTH
Scotland's longest river
begins to widen into its
estuary not far east of the
city of Perth, which owes
its city status not to its size
but to its former role as
the capital of medieval
Scotland.*

town of Kirriemuir, birthplace of J M Barrie, who wrote *Peter Pan*, is the gateway to the Angus glens.

There is sorcery in the River Spey. As it nears the North Sea between the fishing ports of Lossiemouth and Buckie it becomes the fastest flowing river in Britain – but not before it has taken time to assist the production of some of Scotland's finest malt whiskies. Glenfarclas, Glenfiddich, Glen Grant – their names are synonymous with Speyside, and the signposted 'Malt Whisky Trail' conducts you to seven distilleries and a cooperage, each with a visitor centre.

The Spey has all the classic qualities of a Highland river. It rises in the foothills of the Monadhliath Mountains, and the upper valley of Strathspey – strath means valley – has become one of Scotland's major tourist areas; partly for the excellence of its angling, partly for its beauty, and partly for the ski centre of Aviemore, with its access to the high plateau of the Cairngorms.

THE CAIRNGORMS
Their high tableland presents its most formidable face to Strathspey in its precipitous northern corries (above), while the summer aspect of the 'strath' or river valley (opposite) offers gentle walking for those deterred by the wilderness of the plateau with its volatile weather systems.

The naked wilderness of the Cairngorms presides over a gentler landscape of peat-brown water, jewel-like lochs, leafy nature reserves and, in Rothiemurchus, handsome remnants of the Caledonian Forest, the blanket of Scots pine which once covered the Highlands. As the river advances through towns like Grantown-on-Spey and Fochabers its passing is marked by fishing hotels, and when it reaches its estuary the salmon fishing industry is honoured with an exhibition in the Tugnet Ice House, built in 1830 to store ice for packing salmon. Spey Bay marks something of a boundary between the fertile land and sandy coast of the Moray Firth and the plainer, harsher properties of the Aberdeenshire coast as it pushes out into the North Sea.

The Rough and The Smooth

The Seaboard

LOCH KANAIRD AND
BEN MOR COIGACH
The grandeur of the
West Highlands is nowhere
more densely concentrated
than in Wester Ross.

ATLANTIC PUFFIN
A familiar coastline
summer resident.

Scotland has two very different profiles. Its west coast is frayed like a tattered kilt, the land slashed by long sea lochs and piled into rough mountains. The east coast runs smoothly round its firths, lying low in dunes and strands and assertive shelves of cliff. The prevailing features of both seaboards come together in the square-cut north coast.

Although, as the eagle flies, it is only about 275 miles (440 km) from the border with England to the northern edge of the Scottish mainland, the coastline is almost 6200 miles (10,000 km) long. The topography of the west coast is further complicated by the great scatter of the Hebrides, and between the Clyde estuary and Cape Wrath is that heavenly tangle of peak and sea and island which is Scotland's greatest scenic asset.

But the east coast shouldn't be neglected. It is home to most of the country's most famous golf courses, including the Open Championship links at Muirfield, St Andrews and Carnoustie; and in the bays and firths

from Berwickshire to Caithness are some of Scotland's most attractive villages and historic towns. One of them is even English; Berwick-upon-Tweed, which gives its name to Berwickshire, changed hands 13 times in 300 years, and was finally ceded to England in 1482.

The coast north of Berwick is a defiant stretch of cliffs punctuated by rocky fishing harbours. In the marine museum at Eyemouth is a tapestry woven by local people to commemorate the Eyemouth Disaster of 1881, when 189 fishermen were drowned when the fleet foundered in a storm just outside the harbour. At the 300 ft (92 m) outcrop of St Abb's Head, a few miles north, is a nature reserve for one of Scotland's most important seabird colonies.

The red sandstone remnants of its castle are inadequate testament to the history of Dunbar, whose harbour at the mouth of the Firth of Forth made the town strategically important for centuries. England's Edward II fled from the port in 1314, after his comprehensive defeat at Bannockburn. The castle was later overwhelmed and dismantled by Oliver Cromwell, who used its stone to improve the harbour.

Across the Forth estuary is the chunky peninsula of Fife, whose

ST ABBS, BERWICKSHIRE These east-coast cliffs near Eyemouth, just a few miles north of the English border, are home to substantial colonies of seabirds. The wild waters which confront them were responsible for the devastating destruction of the Eyemouth fleet on 14 October 1881, one of Scotland's worst fishing disasters.

ELIE FROM THE AIR, FIFE
With its sandy beaches and protective harbour, Elie is just one of many old fishing villages in this corner of Scotland. The blunt profile of the Kingdom of Fife (the region has retained its historic title) juts into the North Sea between the Firths of Forth and Tay.

northern shore is bounded by the Firth of Tay. Fifers still claim the ancient title of 'Kingdom of Fife' for their region where, until its coal mines closed, heavy industry co-existed with agriculture. Its principal town, Dunfermline, has a palace and abbey (now ruined) closely associated with Scotland's royalty, and was the birthplace of the *émigré* industrialist and philanthropist Andrew Carnegie.

Much of the Fife coast is strung with old fishing villages. The East Neuk, between Elie and Crail, is especially picturesque, but you must round the headland of Fife Ness to find the region's most distinguished town: St Andrews, home to Scotland's oldest university and once the nation's ecclesiastical capital. This ancient settlement by the sea, with its cobbled streets and handsome grey stone, was also the birthplace of Scottish golf (the earliest records date from 1457) and its fine links are internationally dedicated to the game today.

From the mouth of the Tay estuary the coast pushes out into the North Sea in a series of sandy bays, rocky ledges and little ports which in days past had summer lives as resort towns. At Arbroath, the ruined abbey is a potent symbol of Scotland's long struggle for sovereignty. In 1320 Scottish leaders met here to compose and sign

the 'Declaration of Arbroath' – a letter to Pope John XXII which formally asserted Scotland's independence of the English Crown and acknowledged Robert the Bruce as king.

As the coast advances north round the great fist of the Grampians it flags up other landmarks: the vast tidal basin of Montrose, winter home to pink-footed Arctic geese, the shoreline village of Catterline, where the artist Joan Eardley painted some of her stormiest seascapes, and the gaunt ruins of Dunnottar Castle, above Stonehaven, where the Scottish Regalia – 'the Honours of Scotland'– were concealed from Cromwell's Roundheads in the seventeenth century.

The exposed Aberdeenshire coast is unforgiving; its ports are austere and God-fearing and in the crevices of the Buchan cliffs tiny villages cling like limpets to the rocks. Near Peterhead the sea boils into the Bullers o' Buchan, a circular basin of rock which Dr Johnson called 'a monstrous cauldron'.

There are wind-blasted stretches of dune and sand at Balgownie and Newburgh, some elegance in the buildings of Banff and Cullen, and golf to be found at Cruden Bay, where Bram Stoker, the author of *Dracula*, took holidays. It is said that the clifftop ruin of nearby Slains Castle was an inspiration for the Gothic home of the vampire count.

CROVIE, ABERDEENSHIRE
Wedged in between shore and cliff, only the plinth of its main street protects Crovie's houses from the sea.

CRUDEN BAY, ABERDEENSHIRE
The sweeping sands of the bay backs one of the finest links golf courses in Scotland.

More gentle forces have shaped the coast round the Moray Firth, whose southern shores are sandy and flat and spread with pinewoods. Here the land is more sheltered and the climate milder, while the pleasant Morayshire towns of Elgin, Forres and Nairn have sunny reputations. Busy Inverness, in a bowl of hills between the Beauly Firth and the inner basin of the Moray Firth, is the urban epicentre of the Northern Highlands and a major tourist crossroads. From here, travellers either follow the conduit of Loch Ness, the Caledonian Canal and the Great Glen to the West Highland coast, or strike north through Easter Ross to the empty reaches of Caithness and Sutherland, crossing two more firths *en route*.

The complex indents of these firths are worth exploring for the handsome little towns which give them their names, Cromarty and

DUNNET BAY, CAITHNESS

Its windswept arc is pounded by the waters of the Pentland Firth, the boisterous strait which separates the north coast of Scotland from the Orkney Islands. The promontory of nearby Dunnet Head is the northern extremity of mainland Britain – a distinction wrongly claimed by the village of John o' Groats.

Dornoch. Cromarty lies on the eastern point of the Black Isle, which is not an island but a peninsula, and Dornoch with its medieval cathedral is the last substantial settlement before the coast runs through a string of widely spaced villages to the Caithness capital of Wick. This plain but characterful port once harboured a 1000-strong herring fleet and, much earlier, was part of the Caithness fief of the Vikings.

Here the north-east extremity of Scotland is a flat, sharp-edged shelf. The coast between Wick and John o' Groats was one of the earliest inhabited parts of Scotland and the haphazard village of John o' Groats owes its celebrity to its claim to being the northernmost point of Scotland. But that honour goes to Dunnet Head, several miles farther west. John o' Groats offers inviting views across the Pentland Firth to Orkney, and a summer passenger ferry to the island of South Ronaldsay.

From Thurso, once the principal medieval port for trade between Scotland and Scandinavia, the coast sweeps west past the giant dome of the nuclear reprocessing plant at Dounreay to the little townships and free-standing mountains of Sutherland. Shapely Ben Loyal, with its five tops, and startling Ben Hope rise out of rusty peatlands, and the long fissures of the Kyle of Tongue and Loch Eriboll bring intimations of the ragged nature of the western seaboard. At Cape Wrath the coast turns abruptly south, but the cape's name has nothing to do with raging seas. It comes from the norse word *hvarf* which means 'point of turning'.

SUTHERLAND
The region is thinly populated and treasured by walkers of solitary disposition. Here the elegant tops of Ben Loyal rise beyond the Kyle of Tongue (above), while farther west the ruins of Ardvreck Castle haunt the shore of Loch Assynt (below).

Thus begins the glorious littoral of the West Highlands, with its first glimpse of the Hebridean archipelago, and the start of a coastal route which snakes tortuously between hills and round sea lochs, sometimes taking shortcuts by bridge or ferry. Seawards, across the Minch, lie the low profile of Lewis and the humps of Harris, in the Outer Hebrides; landwards the sugarloaf mountains of Sutherland leap from a strange wilderness of glacial boulders and dark water.

WESTER ROSS
The deep fissure of
Loch Broom harbours the
vigorous fishing community
and tourist centre of
Ullapool (above) while
Loch Torridon (below)
bites into the magnificent
Torridon Mountains, whose
stone is among the oldest in
the world.

The landscape of Sutherland and Wester Ross is the loneliest in Scotland, but it wasn't always so. Their glens and straths were once more densely populated, and it is impossible to travel through them without sensing something of the 'Clearances' – a period of Scottish history which saw the forced evacuation of whole communities of crofters in the name of agricultural reform.

When the clan system was dismantled after the failed Jacobite Rebellion of 1745, Highland landowners conspired with Lowland and English farmers to evict their tenants and turn the land over to sheep. The diaspora of the Gael, with mass emigrations to America, Canada and Australia, continued through much of the nineteenth century.

Today, thriving settlements are few and far between. Crofting is only a small part of the local economy and the substantial fishing villages of Lochinver, Ullapool and Gairloch are increasingly dependent on tourism. They now also serve as gateways to such attractive landscapes as Inverpolly National Nature Reserve and the ancient peaks of Torridon.

As the coast continues its fractured progress south the islands of the Inner Hebrides nudge closer, almost touching the mainland at the Kyle narrows where a road bridge now diminishes the island status of the largest and most celebrated: the Isle of Skye. Its great mass and keen profile dominate the lonely littorals of Knoydart, Kintail and Moidart, while the shining shell-sands of Morar, on the 'Road to the Isles,' and the Ardnamurchan peninsula give sublime vistas to the sprawl of lesser isles.

Ardnamurchan Point, with its landmark lighthouse, is the western extremity of the British mainland. The single-track road along Loch Sunart takes two hours to negotiate from the ferry point on Loch Linnhe, and this makes Ardnamurchan even more remote than the nearer islands. Its spare, sea-girt beauty is enchanting, with tiny communities of whitewashed crofthouses scattered along bays of white sand and sheep-cropped turf. The Scottish poet Alasdair Maclean had his roots in Ardnamurchan, and once wrote: 'I have always looked on the ferry which crosses the Narrows of the Linnhe Loch at Corran as a kind of mobile decompression chamber where various kinds of pollution were drained from the blood and I was fitted to breathe pure air again.'

Wide Loch Linnhe bites deeply into the mainland, part of that channel of loch and canal which severs the Highlands from west to

LOCH MORAR, THE SOUND OF SLEAT & ISLAND OF EIGG
These tranquil waters with their view to Eigg – one of the group of four islands called the 'Small Isles' – are alleged to secrete their very own monster. Loch Morar lies on the 'Road to the Isles', the scenic route between Fort William and Mallaig, and although it appears to be part of the seaboard, it is in fact an inland loch of prodigious depth – over 1000 feet. 'Morag', its legendary monster, is said to appear only to foretell the death of a MacDonald of Clanranald.

CASTLE STALKER,
APPIN, ARGYLL
This fourteenth-century
fortress stands on a
prominent site opposite the
northern tip of the island
of Lismore, off the coast of
Loch Linnhe. Although
built by the MacDougalls,
the castle became the
property of the Stewarts of
Appin, whose commitment
to the Jacobite cause
eventually cost them their
lands. Its name is derived
from the Gaelic Stalcair,
which means Hunter.

east and links the towns of Fort William and Inverness. Here the coast remains beautiful but becomes busier, while the major centres of Fort William and Oban are positively urban. Fort William is distinguished for its proximity to Ben Nevis, Britain's highest mountain, while Oban in its delightful wooded bay is the gateway to the Hebrides – the busiest ferry port in the West Highlands.

Southwards the seaboard becomes ever more complex, with great chains of reefs and islets to challenge the sailor. At the yachting haven of Crinan the Crinan Canal cuts through the upper joint of Scotland's longest finger of land – the Knapdale and Kintyre peninsula. This peaceful region has beguiling coastal roads with fine views eastwards to the Clyde estuary and its isles, westwards to the Atlantic and the 'whisky islands' of Islay and Jura.

The towns of the lower Clyde estuary were once the summer playground of urban Scots from the Lowland belt. Today, their resort status has largely succumbed to the lure of foreign holidays, and Wemyss Bay, Largs, Ardrossan and Saltcoats have become either commuter satellites of Glasgow or centres of light industry. The Ayrshire coast, however, has retained a grip on the leisure market,

with championship golf links at Troon and Turnberry and a thriving 'Burns industry' in Alloway which exploits the birthplace and local connections of Scotland's National Bard, Robert Burns.

Between the lower Clyde estuary and the Rhinns of Galloway the coast loses the drama of the West Highland seaboard and becomes more linear. But it doesn't lack interest; among its showpieces are Culzean Castle, magnificently designed by Robert Adam in the late eighteenth century. The castle and its country park are now owned by the National Trust for Scotland, and visitors enjoy the Eisenhower Presentation, which recalls the apartment assigned to the General for his wartime use and, later, his private use for life.

At the head of Loch Ryan is the port of Stranraer, Scotland's main seaport to Northern Ireland. But the coast hasn't quite finished with Scotland. At its impressive extremity are the 200 ft (60 m) cliffs of the Mull of Galloway, within easy view of the Irish coast. From there, it negotiates the deep bays and sandflats of the Solway estuary until, almost imperceptibly, it finds its common frontier with England at the neck of the firth.

EAST LOCH TARBERT, ARGYLL
With its companion West Loch Tarbert, this sea loch almost severs the long finger of the Kintyre peninsula. Kintyre presents splendid views of the Isle of Arran and distant Ayrshire coast, where the championship links at Turnberry (below) attract world-class golfers.

Hebridean Overtures and Norse Sagas

The Islands

ISLAND-HOPPING
Regular ferries service the major islands, including Islay (above, with a view across Loch Gruinart) and Arran (below), in the Clyde estuary, here showing its highest mountain, Goat Fell, and Brodick Bay.

Scotland lays claim to 780 major islands; only the most dedicated cartographers have bothered to count the rash of rocks and sprawl of skerries which constitute the lesser isles. Two of Scotland's principal island groups, Orkney and Shetland, lie off the north coast, and much of their history and culture is rooted in their ancient links with Norway.

The Western Isles, or Outer Hebrides, is the third important group, while the Inner Hebrides – Skye, Mull, Coll, Tiree, Islay, Jura and many more – are magical stepping stones between the mainland and the outer isles. The east coast has no inhabited islands but some spectacular rocks in the Firth of Forth.

There are scheduled air services to Orkney, Shetland and the Western Isles, as well as car and passenger ferry services whose timetables change with the seasons. There are

airstrips on some of the Inner Hebrides, but unless you own or charter a light aircraft they can only be reached in the best way possible: by sea. 'Island-hopping' with the ferries of Caledonian MacBrayne may be a modest form of cruising, but there are few seaways more glorious.

The individual characters of the Inner Hebrides inspire loyalty in locals and visitors alike. Those who love Skye will seldom be persuaded that Mull has much to offer, while the passionately insular will despise both. The two largest islands lie close to the mainland and have the most developed tourist industries. Skye's island status was diminished in 1995 when it was linked to the mainland by a bridge across the Kyle narrows, and a ferry service shuttles between Craignure, on Mull, and the Argyll port of Oban. But even at the height of the tourist season both islands offer plenty of opportunity for solitude and repose – not to mention a strong, sometimes intimidating sense of their essential wilderness.

Skye is blessed and cursed by the specious romance of its history – the flight of Bonnie Prince Charlie after the failed Jacobite Rebellion

THE CUILLIN HILLS & LOCH DÙGHAILL, ISLE OF SKYE
The serrated ridge of Skye's celebrated mountain range is never far from any viewpoint on the West Highland seaboard. The island is the largest of the Inner Hebrides and thanks to song, legend and Jacobite history, the most famous. It is still possible to go 'over the sea to Skye' from two ferry points, but you can now drive onto the island by a toll bridge which spans the narrows at Kyle of Lochalsh.

43

THE CUILLIN RIDGE,
ISLE OF SKYE
The Cuillin Hills pose
perhaps Scotland's most
severe mountaineering
challenge. Deep in their
heart is Loch Coruisk,
which can be reached by
a tourist boat from the
village of Elgol or by an
ambitious walk round the
shores of Loch Scavaig.

of 1745 and his adventures with Flora MacDonald, the Skye gentlewoman who disguised him as her lady's maid and helped him escape to France. There are folk museums, landmarks and memorabilia dedicated to these events, but more eloquent romance to be found in the landscape.

Of all the Hebrides Skye is the most majestic; its Cuillin Hills are the wildest and most precipitous mountains in Britain, and dominate the farthest reaches of the island with their rugged beauty; its seacliffs reach 1000 ft (305 m), with towers of twisted rock formations, and its coast is fissured with narrow sea lochs, bewildering travellers with their tangle of water and land. Such is the convoluted nature of the Skye coastline that no place is more than 5 miles (8 km) from the sea.

The two main population centres are Broadford, which straggles along the shoreline near the Skye Bridge, and the capital, Portree, tucked into a tight bay which is sheltered by the island of Raasay. Both places offer refuge from Skye's uncompromising weather (the Vikings called it Cloud Island) but when the mist lifts there are any number of heart-stopping highlights to inspect: the village of Elgol

with its views to the Small Isles and boat trips to Loch Coruisk, a dark mirror in a bowl of Cuillins, the Trotternish Peninsula with the weird pinnacles of the Quiraing, Dunvegan Castle, seat of the MacLeods, and the high headland of Neist Point, where Skye looks across the Minch to the Outer Hebrides... an inexhaustible range of spectacular viewpoints.

Mull is greener and more wooded than Skye, but there is desolation too, in the hills of Glen More and the wild coast of the Ross of Mull, the long finger of land which reaches into the Atlantic. Mull's capital is the prettiest port in Scotland: Tobermory, whose brightly painted waterfront houses were purpose-built in the late eighteenth century by the British Fisheries Society. Leafy Tobermory Bay is one of the safest anchorages in the West Highlands, and in 1588 it offered refuge to a galleon of the Spanish Armada, whose sunken treasure has been unsuccessfully hunted by generations of divers.

Mull has other claims on history, not least its connections with a small offshore island at the tip of the Ross. To reach Iona,

ROSS OF MULL, & ARDMEANACH, ISLE OF MULL
Mull's many attractions may lure a great number of visitors every year, but the island never loses the solitude of its landscape or the grandeur of its coastline.

TOBERMORY, ISLE OF MULL

IONA

In the summer months beachcombers and pilgrims vie for possession of the island which was the centre of the Christian world in the sixth century. Its shining strands seem to have their own spiritual qualities, whilst the abbey founded by St Columba remains a shrine today.

one of the major Christian shrines, you must first pass through Mull, tracing the footsteps of generations of pilgrims and the early cortèges of Scottish monarchs. Iona's sacred reputation made it the burial ground for Scottish royalty, and visitors follow the ancient funeral route through Glen More to the shores of Loch Scridain and, finally, the little harbour of Fionnphort.

There a passenger ferry crosses the Sound of Iona in 10 minutes, depositing half a million passengers a year on the tiny island where Saint Columba landed in 563. Here, with 12 companions from his native Ireland, he established the mission which turned Iona into the Christian centre of Europe. The restored abbey with its royal graveyard (almost 50 European kings, chieftains and Lords of the Isles are said to be buried there) is now the focus of attention, but many are just as touched by the simple beauty of Iona and its atmosphere of peace.

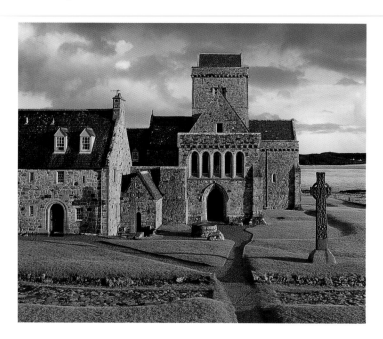

From Fionnphort and other harbours on Mull you can take boat trips to the uninhabited Treshnish Isles, with their bird and seal colonies, and the island of Staffa, where the columnar basalt of Fingal's

Cave, like giant organ pipes, was an inspiration for Mendelssohn's Hebridean Overture. If the seas and tides permit, passengers are landed on the island to take a thrilling walk into the great maw of the cave and inspect its formations at close quarters.

West of Mull are the sister islands of Coll and Tiree, the former only slightly less flat than the latter, whose Gaelic name means 'land below the waves.' Like Colonsay to the south, they are crofting islands which have summer populations of devoted visitors: families who return each year to turn their children loose on unblemished beaches and, on gusty Tiree, surfers who ride the Atlantic rollers onto miles of pale shell sand.

TRÁIGH NAN GILEAN, TIREE
Tiree is reputed to be the sunniest as well as the windiest island in the Western Isles. It has recently found a new niche in the leisure market as a venue for surfing competitions.

To the north, sheltered by the arm of Ardnamurchan and the bulk of Skye, are the four Small Isles, whose fans believe them the most enchanting. Each certainly has its own personality, and to sample the different characters of Eigg, Rum, Muck and Canna, you can take the seven-hour 'Small Isles Cruise' which is actually their ferry service from the fishing port and railhead of Mallaig. The ferry makes the round trip daily, except Sundays, in summer, and four times a week in winter; if you complete the circuit you won't have any time on shore, but there are few finer sails on the West Highland seaboard.

The other major islands of the Inner Hebrides are Islay and Jura,

*CALANAIS STANDING
STONES, LEWIS
Erected between 3000 and
1500 BC, the mysterious
stones of Calanais form
one of the most significant
prehistoric sites in Britain.
Besides the central ring
of 13 megaliths there
are a further 35 stones in
their vicinity. The complex,
with its chambered cairn,
is located some 15 miles
(24 km) from Stornoway,
which is the principal town
of Lewis, as well as the
administrative capital
of the Outer Hebrides.*

which lie some distance south of the main group and are reached
from West Loch Tarbert, on the Kintyre peninsula. Jura, smaller but
higher than Islay, is thinly populated, and the three striking Paps of
Jura are among the shapeliest mountains in Scotland. It has two other
claims to popular fame: George Orwell wrote *1984* in an isolated
house at the north end of the island, and the Strait of Corrievreckan,
between Jura and Scarba, is notorious for whirlpools and tidal races.

Islay is almost urban by comparison, with eight distinguished
distilleries which underpin its farming and fishing economy.
Bowmore, Lagavulin, Laphroaig – their names are magic to the ears
of connoisseurs of malt whisky. The island's population is over 4000,
most of it centred on Port Ellen, Bowmore and Port Charlotte, and
its beaches, golf, bird life and early Christian sites provide plenty of
interest for visitors, who can tour the distilleries on rainy days.

Some 40 miles (64 km) from the mainland, the Outer Hebrides
represent the outer edge. Like the rest of the Hebrides, they were
formed during the Ice Age when the western seaboard of Scotland
subsided suddenly, leaving mountain tops in the sea. For many, the

bare peatlands and minimalist landscape of this close-linked archipelago are an acquired taste, but their isolation has made them the last redoubt of the Gàidhealtachd – the land of the Gael. You will hear Gaelic spoken elsewhere in the Hebrides but you will hear it most between the Butt of Lewis and Barra Head.

In the 130 miles (210 km) between these two points is the Long Island, as the Vikings called the island chain which, thanks to a series of causeways and bridges, has indeed become almost unbroken. Lewis and Harris (home of the cottage industry which produces Harris Tweed) are the largest and most northerly, and have traditionally been called two islands. But geographically they are one. Their frontier is defined not by the sea but by the mountains of Harris.

On the other side of the range is Tarbert, which sits on a neck of land between two sea lochs. They bite so deeply into the land they almost meet, and the isthmus just prevents the detachment of South Harris from North Harris. At the mouth of East Loch Tarbert is the island of Scalpay, which succoured Bonnie Prince Charlie on his melancholy, inter-island flight from Culloden, and to the north are

LUSKENTYRE BEACH, HARRIS
The west coast of Harris confronts the Atlantic Ocean, where only a scatter of uninhabited islands stand between it and the North American coast. Harris and Lewis are part of the same island but the high Harris hills, pictured here, mark the frontier with low-lying Lewis to the North.

ST KILDA
This archipelago is the most isolated and westerly of the Outer Hebrides. The main island of Hirta was inhabited for almost 4000 years until its evacuation in 1930. Its landscape harbours the highest sea-cliffs and stacks in Britain and is home to vast seabird colonies.

mountains with peaks between 2000 and 3000 ft (610 and 914 m). Much of South Harris is a wilderness of rock, heather and lochans, but its Atlantic coast is scooped into vast arcs of shining sand.

The greatest glory of the Outer Hebrides is their beaches. Like Harris and Lewis, the other main islands in the chain – North Uist, Benbecula, South Uist and Barra – are almost bereft of trees, and many people find this austere landscape discomfiting. But for lovers of 'naked nature', as Dr Johnson put it, the beaches beguile with their sheep-cropped machair, white sand and aquamarine shallows, with the finest strands facing into the Atlantic, where the only land between Scotland and Newfoundland is St Kilda, 45 miles (72 km) to the west.

A World Heritage Site, this lonely island group once supported a population of crofters and fishermen, who scraped a living from precipitous fields and the seabird colonies of mighty, 1000 ft (305 m) cliffs. By 1930 life had become too difficult for them, and the surviving population of 35 were evacuated to the mainland at their own request. Today, St Kilda is owned by the National Trust for Scotland and supports merely the world's largest colony of gannets, as well as thousands of fulmars and puffins.

Scenically, the Northern Isles have much in common with many

of their Hebridean counterparts. Orkney and Shetland, substantial island groups separated by 60 miles (96 km) of sea, are well nigh treeless, and the seaboards of both are pierced by sea lochs and teased into a perplexing jigsaw of water and land. But there the resemblance ends – to the Hebrides and each other.

Orkney, which lies just 6 miles (10 km) across the Pentland Firth from the Scottish mainland, is green, low-lying and fertile; Shetland's peat-brown uplands are desolate. Both groups, who confusingly call their principal island Mainland, were annexed to Norway in 875 and governed by their own Norse earls until 1468. This period has left an enduring imprint on the islands, their dialects and their people, for whom Norse sagas and Viking history are more significant than the culture of the Gael.

Although it is known that both archipelagos were settled in the Stone Age and later colonised by the Picts, it is Orkney which is the treasure house of these times, with the densest concentration of prehistoric monuments in Britain. From the magnificent chambered tomb of Maes Howe to the great Ring of Brogar and the Stone-Age village of Skara Brae, Orkney is paradise for archaeologists – amateur or otherwise.

ORKNEY
The island of Hoy with its singular rock stack the 'Old Man of Hoy' (above), is the highest island in the low-lying Orkney group. These northern isles are endowed with many prehistoric sites, including Skara Brae (below) the best-preserved Neolithic village in Europe.

YELL SOUND, SHETLAND
You are never far from the sea in the Shetland Islands.

MOUSA BROCH, SHETLAND
Mousa Broch is the finest surviving Iron Age broch tower in Scotland. It stands on the now uninhabited island of Mousa, off the east shore of the South Mainland.

In its capital and main port, Kirkwall, is its most splendid antiquity of the Norse period: the twelfth-century masterpiece of St Magnus Cathedral, which entertains an annual festival of classical music. Nearby are the ruins of the Bishop's Palace where Haakon Haakonson, Norway's greatest king, lay dying in the thirteenth century while his courtiers comforted him by reciting Norse sagas. Among these 70 verdant islands, of which under a third are inhabited, there are any number of other relics to explore, including some poignant testaments to Orkney's strategic naval role in the Second World War.

Both Orkney and Shetland have shared some of the economic benefits of the North Sea oil industry, but Shetland seized the main prize with the development of Sullom Voe, the 1000-acre (400 ha) terminal in the south of Mainland which receives half of Britain's oil production. The shrewd Shetlanders forced the oil companies to make this huge development as friendly as possible to its rural site, and with over 80 uninhabited islands in its 100-strong group Shetland certainly had room to spare.

With so much unproductive land (sheep and Shetland knitwear

notwithstanding) it has always relied more heavily on the harvests of the sea, despite the fierce nature of the cliff-bound coast which, in the nature reserves of Hermaness and Noss, provides ornithologists with some of their rarest seabird sightings. And although Shetland lacks the scale and richness of Orkney's prehistoric sites, Mousa Broch, which is only accessible by boat during the summer months, is the best-preserved of its kind in Britain.

Shetland has maintained its Norse heritage even more strenuously than Orkney. The unusual Shetland dialect uses many words of Norse origin, and the lively port of Lerwick, the capital, gets much of its traffic from Scandinavia and the Baltic states. But Shetland's Viking legacy reaches its apotheosis each January in the pagan fire festival of Up Helly Aa, when the return of the sun is welcomed by a procession of latterday 'Vikings' bearing flaming torches, and the burning of a replica galley. Up Helly Aa remains very much a local event. Shetlanders are too friendly to be unwelcoming, but this dramatic festival makes no concessions to tourism. The creative insularity of an island people has helped preserve its traditions.

*ESHANESS,
NORTH MAINLAND,
SHETLAND
Shetland's most complex island topography is further complicated by narrow sounds and fjord-like sea lochs. Here winter defines the austere landscape of the North Mainland, where Shetland's traditional economies of fishing, farming and knitwear are now underpinned by the North Sea oil industry. Like Orkney, Scotland's most northerly island group was once part of the kingdom of Norway, and Norse influences remain strong.*

Highland Highlights

The Best of the Rest

Almost everyone who visits Scotland for the first time will find the familiar in its Highland landscape. Images of Scotland – rugged mountains, lonely glens, tranquil lochs, heroic castles – have gone round the world on shortbread tins, calendars and whisky labels. Yet such is the theatrical diversity of the Scottish climate that the reality strikes the visitor with a shock of novelty. There is no single Loch Lomond, Glencoe, Eilean Donan Castle; their personalities are multiple, and their spectacle changes with the light, the seasons and – if the weather is volatile – the hours of the day.

The most famous set pieces of the Highland landscape are not always the most beautiful. Some owe their celebrity to song or poem, some to history, and some to legend. Loch Ness is impressive for its scale, but it is fixed on the tourist itinerary for its Monster. The elusive 'Nessie', who may or may not exist, has become not merely an icon but the subject of serious scientific research.

You can cruise the 24-mile (38-km) long loch on excursions from Inverness at the north end and Fort Augustus at the south. At Drumnadrochit is the Official Loch Ness Exhibition, which displays the photographic evidence of the Nessie phenomenon and discusses some of the current theories on its origin.

The Inverness area has other icons. Five miles (8 km) from the

URQUHART CASTLE & LOCH NESS
Overlooking Loch Ness, Urquhart Castle occupies a strategic site in the Great Glen. The original castle dates from around the twelfth century, but the ruins we see today were largely constructed in the sixteenth century.

HEATHER MOORLAND & THE CAIRNGORM MOUNTAINS (opposite)
Heather is not only a symbol of Scotland, but the most prolific plant to be found on its hills. High season for heather is the months of August and September when its rich purple flowers come into bloom.

GLENCOE

Few landscapes live up to their reputations more dramatically than the deep gash and grim mountains of Glencoe, which has become synonymous with the most notorious act of Highland treachery. In truth, more people died in other brutal slayings throughout Scotland's savage history, but the nature of the 'Massacre of Glencoe' has given it special infamy.

town is the melancholy site of Culloden Battlefield: the place which, on 16 April 1746, not only ended Bonnie Prince Charlie's hopes of recovering the British Crown for the exiled Stewart dynasty but precipitated the dismantling of the Highland clan system. Led by the Duke of Cumberland the government forces, which included many Lowland Scots, met the Jacobite army of Charles Edward Stewart on Culloden Moor, and routed them in an afternoon.

Part shrine, part war grave, part military museum, the site is an atmospheric place. The misplaced heroism of the exhausted, ill-equipped Jacobite army is eloquently evoked by the Graves of the Clans – a scatter of simple stones bearing the names of each clan, said to mark the spot where they fell.

The tribal feudalism of the clan system was, in fact, long overdue for reform, but the brutal nature of its repression after Culloden (the wearing of tartan and the speaking of Gaelic were proscribed) guaranteed immortality for the Highlander. From then on, he moved swiftly from tragic victim to romantic hero to stalwart of the British state, whose masterstroke was to dress him again in tartan, restore his bagpipes and send him to war in the service of the Empire.

There is another corner of the Highlands indelibly imprinted with infamous events: Glencoe. The Massacre of Glencoe predates Culloden but was part of the same struggle between clan and Crown – between sympathisers of the deposed Stewarts and supporters of the

new royal order. In a savage winter dawn in 1692 government soldiers of the Argyll Campbells fell upon their hosts, the MacDonalds, and slaughtered 40 members of the clan; many of those who fled into the hills later died of cold.

The Glencoe mountains are notorious for other reasons. They still claim lives; their cliffs and ridges are among Britain's most severe mountaineering challenges. The north face of Ben Nevis, some 15 miles (24 km) to the north, is also a supreme test but the 4409 feet (1344 m) of Britain's highest mountain is easily climbed by approaches from the beautiful wooded gorge of Glen Nevis.

West of Ben Nevis and Fort William is another glen whose name resonates down the centuries: Glenfinnan, where Bonnie Prince Charlie raised the Stewart banner to the Jacobite cause. The short-lived adventure of the '45 was underway. A baroque column topped with a bearded Highlander marks its starting point. Glenfinnan's other distinctive landmark is the railway viaduct which carries

BEN NEVIS
At 4409 ft (1344 m) Ben Nevis is Britain's highest mountain.

GLENFINNAN VIADUCT
The train crosses this landmark at Glenfinnan, where Bonnie Prince Charlie raised his standard in 1745.

ROYAL DEESIDE
Balmoral Castle on the River Dee (above) has been the summer home of the royal family since Queen Victoria.

CASTLE FRASER, ABERDEENSHIRE
dates from 1575 and is just one of the many historic castles found in the region.

trains between Glasgow and Mallaig on the West Highland Line.

Many of Scotland's glens, like its lochs and castles, have reputations which compete for scenic supremacy. Some, like Glen Shiel in Kintail and Glen Torridon in Wester Ross, back their claims with mountain grandeur, wild and uncompromising. Others, like Glen Lyon in Perthshire, Glen Feshie in the Cairngorms, and Glen Affric, west of Inverness, have more subtle qualities: green straths by salmon rivers or glassy lochs, handsome hills and broadleaf woodland and the rusty boles and dark canopies of great pine trees – survivors of the ancient Caledonian Forest which once blanketed the Highlands.

Other beauty spots acquire celebrity through their visitors. The Dee valley has splendid scenery and a salmon river, but it earned its soubriquet 'Royal Deeside' through the patronage of Queen Victoria, who bought the Balmoral estate in 1852. Imposing Balmoral Castle, which was rebuilt in Scottish baronial style on Prince Albert's initiative, remains the summer home of the royal family, and the dignified town of Ballater, which was a spa

town in the nineteenth century, is their local shopping centre.

Between Aberdeen and Braemar is an attractive string of castles, towns and villages that follow the course of the Dee through its pastoral lower valley to the wild uplands of the Grampians. The valley's side attractions, like Glen Tanar and the Muir of Dinnet, are also worth exploring, and beyond Braemar the youthful river squeezes itself through the dramatic gorge of the Linn of Dee. This is prime walking country, with routes to the 3786 ft (1154 m) summit of Lochnagar and access to the popular Cairngorm pass of the Lairig Ghru.

At the southern end of the Highlands, at their interface with the Lowlands, is another area famous as much for its associations as its beauty: the Trossachs, a region of rumpled hills and gem-like lochs which became a touchstone of the romantic wilderness for poets like Wordsworth, whose interest was inspired by the novels of Sir Walter Scott. The Trossachs were also the home territory of Rob Roy MacGregor, guerrilla fighter, cattle thief, folk hero and Highland gentleman. (He was Captain of Clan Appin, but as the second son of their chieftain never became chief himself.)

The Trossachs' western boundary is the largest body of fresh water in the British Isles. It isn't only the sentiments of a much-loved song which have given Loch Lomond its popularity, but its proximity to

THE TROSSACHS
This rich concentration of hills, forests and lochs represents a last flourish of Highland landscape before it subsides into the Lowlands to the south. The Trossachs leapt to popularity in Victorian times and visitors to Loch Katrine (above) can still take trips on the paddle-steamer, SS Sir Walter Scott. Loch Achray (below) is enclosed by the woodlands of Queen Elizabeth Forest Park.

LIATHACH,
TORRIDON,
WESTER ROSS.
The overwhelming bulk
of Liathach rears above
the village of Torridon.
With its companion peaks,
Beinn Alligin and Beinn
Eighe, it forms a mountain
group which is one of
the most impressive in
the West Highlands.

Glasgow. However, the beauty and sheer scale of Loch Lomond – it is 22 miles (35 km) long and 5 miles (8 km) broad at its widest point – manage to transcend its hustle and bustle. Its east shore, dominated by Ben Lomond and protected by the Queen Elizabeth Forest Park, is especially handsome, and as the loch narrows towards its northern tip the surrounding mountains become more and more steep.

There are two other claimants to the title of Scotland's most beautiful inland loch and, like Loch Lomond, they are both distinguished by their islands. One is Loch Maree, which is the centrepiece of a magnificent region of Wester Ross. Twelve miles (19 km) long, Loch Maree's highlights include remnants of the Caledonian pine forest, a serene shoreline of mixed woodland and waterfalls, the great mountain of Slioch, which is almost free-standing, and enchanting views across the cluster of isles at its widest part.

But Loch Maree is also within easy striking distance of some of Scotland's most breathtaking scenery: the ancient Torridon mountains, with their formidable triptych of Beinn Alligin, Liathach and Beinn Eighe, the roadless Fisherfield Forest, where there are few trees but several of the Highlands' most isolated peaks, and the glorious shores of Gair Loch, Gruinard Bay and Loch Ewe, where an unexpected attraction is the sub-tropical eco-system of Inverewe Gardens.

Loch Awe is the longest inland loch in the south-west Highlands. The 23 miles (37 km) of its narrow waters almost form

a channel between central Argyll and the west coast. The scenery is more pastoral and peaceful at its southern end, while northern Loch Awe is almost overwhelmed by the massive bulk of Ben Cruachan, whose 3695 ft (1126 m) summit can be reached from the Pass of Brander, an intimidating gash where the loch becomes the River Awe. (The pass still looks like the perfect spot for an ambush, as it once was; Robert the Bruce fought the Clan MacDougal there in 1308.) Cruachan is host to a pumped-storage power station buried deep in the heart of the mountain, which the public can visit on tours through the access tunnel.

The most romantic feature of Loch Awe, however, is Kilchurn Castle, an elegant ruin which stands on a spit of land on the loch's north-east arm, where the sheltered water mirrors its reflection. Kilchurn was built in 1440 by Sir Colin Campbell of Glen Orchy, an ancestor of the Breadalbane family, who inhabited the castle for the next 300 years. In the aftermath of the Jacobite Rebellion of 1745 it became a garrison for Hanoverian troops, and it was finally abandoned and fell into ruin after it was struck by lightning and lost part of a tower.

LOCH AWE AND KILCHURN CASTLE, ARGYLL
An overview of Loch Awe, Scotland's longest inland loch, shows Kilchurn Castle on a little peninsula at its north end. Scotland's fortresses come in many sizes and most conditions, and for castle connoisseurs who prefer the ruined to the restored there are few more elegant remnants than the walls and towers of Kilchurn.

EILEAN DONAN CASTLE, LOCH DUICH

Scotland's castles begin and end with Eilean Donan, a fortress which has appeared on more calendars, postcards, tea cloths, shortbread tins, and whisky labels than any other. Why? Perhaps because, more than any other, it represents a kind of universal Scotland – isolated but accessible, grim but dignified and more than anything, scenically theatrical. If Eilean Donan Castle is Scotland's pre-eminent visual cliché then its unique site and glorious setting have conspired to make it so. And it has earned its place in the iconology of global landmarks.

If Kilchurn and its site offer a poetic image of melancholy Highland beauty, the impact of Eilean Donan Castle is more heroic. Eilean Donan's majestic situation and defiant profile make it a stock symbol of Scotland throughout the world, and all who see it for the first time can't help feeling they've known it in another life.

The castle occupies its own islet at the confluence of Loch Duich, Loch Alsh and Loch Long, on the mainland opposite Skye. It has been there since 1220, but owes its complete appearance and habitable condition to a restoration in the nineteenth century. In its time it has been a deterrent to Viking invasion, a stronghold of the Mackenzie earls of Seaforth, a temporary garrison for Spanish soldiers and more recently, a museum of Jacobite relics.

Few fortresses play the part more satisfyingly than Eilean Donan, against a backdrop of mountain and sea. Its weathered walls, battlements and turrets look impregnable; but in the first round of Jacobite unrest it was blown to bits by a Hanoverian warship, and left in ruins for nearly 200 years.

Like the great castles of Edinburgh and Stirling on their defensive rocks, there are grim aspects to Eilean Donan. But not all Scottish castles lack grace. The golden age of castle architecture was the late sixteenth and seventeenth centuries, and its most productive heartland was Aberdeenshire, which is rich in fortified 'tower houses' – the distinctive style which produced such fairy-tale citadels as Crathes Castle on Deeside, and Craigievar Castle, which lies between the Dee and the Don.

Among the most visited castles are the seats of the Dukes of Argyll and the Dukes of Atholl – historically, two of the most powerful families in Scotland. The Duke of Argyll is the chief of Clan Campbell, and Inverary Castle has been the family seat since it was built on the banks of Loch Fyne in 1745 – the year of the second Jacobite rebellion. The Campbells were persistent opponents of the Jacobite cause, and the scale of Inverary's Gothic exterior and splendour of its interior indicate the rewards of backing the winning side.

Whitewashed Blair Castle looks like a huge snowdrift which has detached itself from the Perthshire mountains and slid into Glen Garry, north of the Pass of Killiecrankie. It, too, is a substantial edifice – despite the fact that the Jacobite Duke of Atholl backed the losing side. Parts of this sprawling Scottish baronial mansion are 700 years old, while the eighteenth-century wing cherishes such treasures as the gloves and pipe of Bonnie Prince Charlie, who spent two days in the castle drumming up support.

One hundred years after the '45 rebellion, Queen Victoria visited Blair Castle and endowed the Dukes of Atholl with the right to maintain a private army. This small force remains the only private army in Britain today, but unlike their Jacobite ancestors the Atholl Highlanders have never taken up arms against the Crown. Thus the British state tames and recruits its rebels.

BLAIR CASTLE,
PERTHSHIRE
Ancestral home of the
Dukes of Atholl.

INVERARY CASTLE,
ARGYLL
Family seat of the chiefs
of Clan Campbell.

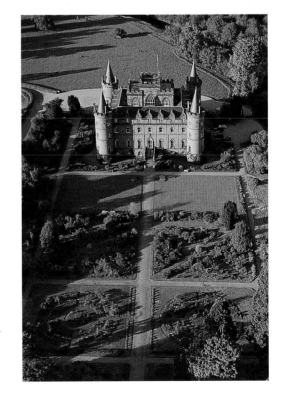

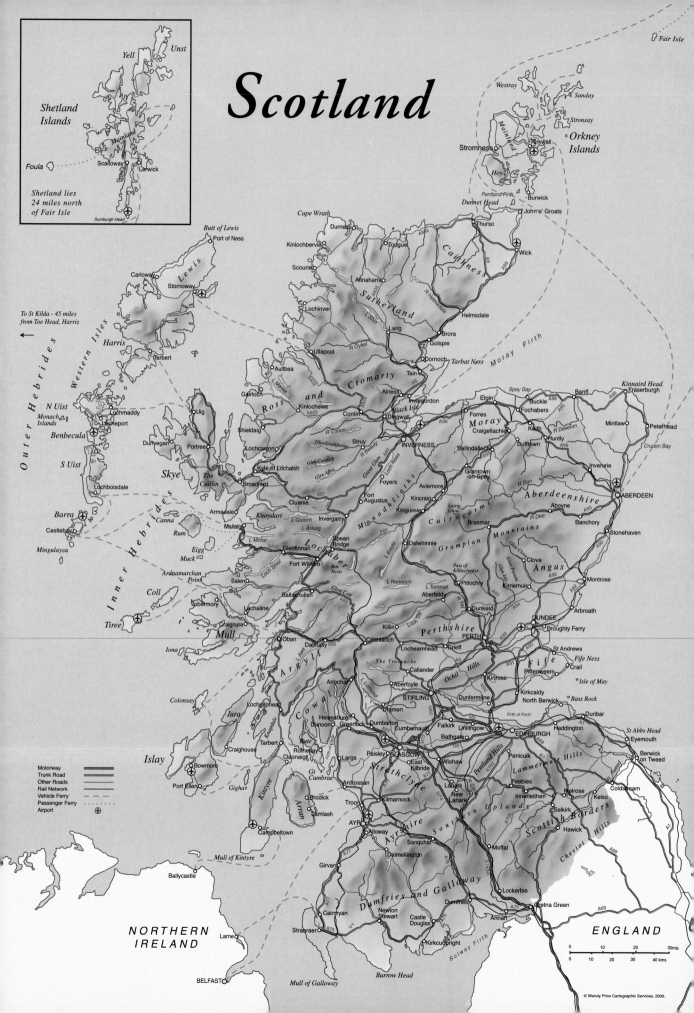

Scotland

Shetland Islands

Unst
Yell

Foula

Mainland

Scalloway • Lerwick

Shetland lies
24 miles north
of Fair Isle

Sumburgh Head

Fair Isle

Westray
Sanday
Stronsay

Mainland

Stromness • Kirkwall — **Orkney Islands**

Hoy

Burwick

Pentland Firth

Dunnet Head
John o' Groats

Cape Wrath

Durness
Tongue
Thurso
Wick

Kinlochbervie
Scourie
Altnaharra
Caithness
A9

Butt of Lewis
Port of Ness

Carloway
Lewis
Stornoway

To St Kilda - 45 miles
from Toe Head, Harris

Lochinver
R Shin
Lairg
Helmsdale
Brora
Golspie

Sutherland

R Oykel

Ullapool

Harris
Tarbert

Aultbea
Gairloch
Kinlochewe
Ross and Cromarty
Contin
Dornoch
Tarbat Ness
Tain
Alness
Invergordon
Black Isle
Dingwall
Moray Firth

Western Isles

Outer Hebrides

N Uist
Monach Islands
Lochmaddy
Locheport

Benbecula

S Uist

Lochboisdale

Shieldaig
Lochcarron
Dunvegan
Portree
Skye
Kyle of Lochalsh
The Cuillin
Broadford

Glen Strathfarrar
R Conon
Struy
R Beauly
Glen Cannich
Glen Affric
INVERNESS

Elgin
Forres
Spey Bay
Buckie
Fochabers
A98
Banff
Kinnaird Head
Fraserburgh

Moray
Craigellachie
Keith
R Deveron
Huntly
Dufftown
Mintlaw
Peterhead

Ballindalloch
A96
Cruden Bay
Inverurie

Great Glen
Loch Ness
Foyers
Grantown-on-Spey
Fort Augustus
Aviemore
Aberdeenshire
Kincraig
Kingussie
ABERDEEN
Aboyne

Barra
Castlebay

Inner Hebrides
Canna
Rum
Eigg
Muck

Armadale
Knoydart
L Quoich
Invergarry
L Arkaig
Monadhliaths
Cairngorms
Lairig Ghru
Braemar
R Dee
Banchory
Stonehaven

Mingulay

Ardnamurchan Point

Mallaig
L Morar
Glenfinnan
Spean Bridge
Lochaber
Loch Shiel
Fort William
Ben Nevis
Salen

Dalwhinnie
L Ericht
Grampian Mountains
Glen Clova
Clova
Angus
Kirriemuir
Montrose

Coll

Tobermory
Lochaline
Mull
Craignure
Iona

Ballachulish
Glen Coe
A82
Killin
Loch Tay
L Rannoch
L Tummel
Pass of Killiecrankie
Pitlochry
Aberfeldy
R Tay
Dunkeld
Arbroath
Broughty Ferry
DUNDEE

Oban
Dalmally
R Awe
Crianlarich
Lochearnhead
Crieff
PERTHSHIRE
PERTH
St Andrews
Fife Ness
Crail

Argyll
The Trossachs
Callander
Ochil Hills
Kinross
Pittenweem
Isle of May

L Lomond
Aberfoyle
Fife
Kirkcaldy
North Berwick
Bass Rock

Jura
Lochgilphead
Cowal
Arrochar
Drymen
STIRLING
Dunfermline

Colonsay

Helensburgh
Dunoon
Greenock
Dumbarton
Cumbernauld
Falkirk
Linlithgow
Bathgate
EDINBURGH
Haddington
St Abbs Head
Eyemouth

Islay
Craighouse

Bute
Rothesay
Paisley
GLASGOW
Wishaw
East Kilbride
Peebles
Lammermuir Hills
Pentland Hills
Penicuik
Berwick on Tweed

Bowmore
Port Ellen
Gigha

Tarbert
Claonaig
Largs
Gt Cumbrae
Lanark
New Lanark
Innerleithen
Melrose
Kelso
Coldstream

Kintyre
Brodick
Ardrossan
Kilmarnock
Strathclyde
Peebles
Selkirk
Scottish Borders
Hawick

Arran
Lamlash
Troon
AYR
Alloway
Ayrshire
Sanquhar
Moffat
Southern Uplands
Cheviot Hills

Campbeltown

Ballycastle

Girvan
Dalmellington
Dalmellington

Mull of Kintyre

Cairnryan
Dumfries and Galloway
Newton Stewart
Castle Douglas
Lockerbie
Gretna Green

Stranraer
Kirkcudbright
Dumfries
Annan
A75

Larne

NORTHERN IRELAND

BELFAST

Mull of Galloway
Burrow Head
Solway Firth

ENGLAND

Motorway
Trunk Road
Other Roads
Rail Network
Vehicle Ferry
Passenger Ferry
Airport

0   10   20   30mls
0 10 20 30 40kms

© Wendy Price Cartographic Services. 2000.